THE STORY OF A GARDENING NOBODY

by

WALTER WILDE

Walter Wilde

The Bassett Press

First published in 2002 and typeset by:

The Bassett Press
61 Glen Eyre Road
Southampton
SO16 3NP

ISBN 1 873633 04 1

British Library Cataloguing in Publication Data. A catalogue record for this book is available from The British Library.

Printed in Great Britain by Hobbs The Printers Limited,
Brunel Road, Totton, Hampshire. SO40 3YS

For my family including
Paddy and Jacob who are
both now with the stars.

ACKNOWLEDGEMENTS

The author gives grateful thanks to

Barbara Hopkinson for skilful typing of the manuscript;

Gordon Bloomer, of the Bassett Press, for invaluable editorial help.

Thanks are also given to Barbara Lea Taylor for permission to quote from her New Zealand Article and to Erika R. Shank and Rossa W. Cole for photographs of the author taken in Ireland and New York.

CONTENTS

ILLUSTRATIONS

Introduction

This is a very ordinary tale of a very ordinary gardener who has been obsessed with nature, plants, personalities and garden styles for at least six decades. It starts with a boy walking along the Great North Road between Newark-on-Trent and South Muskham to tend a tiny cottage plot. And after National Service and Cambridge University the story continues to Blackpool, Hereford, Walsall and a Worcestershire village. The education of this gardening nobody includes annuals, perennials, shrubs, especially camellias, and an allotment. It ends with a labour saving garden. In between, travels to many tropical lands provide stimuli and illustrations for many lectures at home and abroad on ecosystems and on gardens.

Perhaps reading Geography at Cambridge fostered a 'buoyant and ebullient eclecticism'. To counteract this trait, research into Landscape Parks focussed on the minutiae of eighteenth century landscapes. It also created an abiding admiration for great personalities such as Capability Brown

(1716-1783), whose genius I am constantly defending against narrow-minded and prejudiced academics who merely regard him as a mercenary 'minimalist'. He was, along with Joseph Paxton in the nineteenth century, a very great all-round gardener.

From 1972 to the present time I have had the great pleasure of running courses in Garden History at Birmingham University and other West Midland Centres. These had initially what one kindly colleague called a 'heroic approach' but over the years they have grown in detail, intensity and scope. The average attendance of 25 class members over a 30-year period never ceases to amaze and delight me.

How I wish I could emulate the late E. B. Anderson in his 'Seven Gardens or Sixty Years of Gardening' (M. Joseph, 1973) but his horticultural knowledge was vastly superior to my own. As a lecturer, however, I am told that I have succeeded in 'instructing, delighting and moving' many audiences to greater enjoyment in visiting gardens and a richer delight in gardening in their own paradise.

Chapter 1: EARLY DAYS

It was perfectly safe to walk alone along the Great North Road to South Muskham in the mid-1930s. No juggernauts thundered past the sugar beet factory and so I was able to collect fallen beet from the kerb with safety. These were for the pig which my grandparents kept at Jasmine Cottage. As I crossed the River Trent I would often digress into the fields and watch kingfishers nesting in the sandy banks of the river and swallows swooping under the arches. Biodiversity was the norm and since the farmers did not spray their fields there were huge drifts of wild flowers. Cowslips were my favourite and, as E. A. Bowles once said, 'If heaven has a smell, let it be of cowslips.'

The hedgerows were full of birds nests, especially greenfinches. And scribble larks or yellow-hammers nested at regular intervals in the base of wild rose bushes. Today the countryside by comparison is dead, killed by present farm practices, fertilisers, pesticides, hedge removals and subsidies.

As I walked the two and a half miles to South Muskham I knew of copses where wild violets and primroses grew in abundance and of ponds full of newts and bulrushes (reed mace). And I was in no hurry to reach Jasmine Cottage near the village church where my grandparents had given me a small plot to grow the plants I loved. In 1934 I was seven years old and had been brought up by a loving mother and father through every illness imaginable. And when we moved from a small terrace house in Cliff Nook Lane to a Georgian house in Middle Gate, Newark-on-Trent, we were adjacent to the fine old Castle where the Al and the A46 crossed. From here it was due North to my grandparents' cottage. Nearby was the level crossing where main line trains thundered northwards. As they did so they picked up water and I enjoyed the spray being blown into my face. Beyond were the meanders of watercourses abandoned by the Trent in an area called The Fleet. The lush grass had Lady's smock (*cardamine praetensis*) and marsh marigolds (*calthra palustris*) in drifts and in the pollarded willows wild ducks nested. I once took some eggs for my grandmother to bake in a cherry cake.

My grandparents were Pinchbecks from Wrangle in Lincolnshire. They worked incredibly hard from dawn to dusk. 'Genteel, but impoverished' might describe my grandmother who was loved by everyone in the village. She worshipped at North Muskham Methodist Chapel, whilst my grandfather was a Church of England Steward. Indeed he was once sidesman at Caunton where Dean Hole the famous Rosarian had once been vicar.

The Pinchbecks moved to Jasmine Cottage in 1924 and I remember my grandfather ploughing adjacent fields with two magnificent Shire horses. As I was allowed to ride on their backs I remembered marvelling at these wonderful animals which I trust will never die out.

Between the pigsty and the *Charles Ross* apple tree was my small plot and in this five by two metre area I crammed the perennials I liked. As my grandfather pleached everything into domes the laurel bush gave dense shade at the northern end of this area and at the other end a bush of Lad's Love (Artemisia) produced a pungent smell when disturbed. All told, this plot was rather shady and would certainly not have received the approval of Jane Loudon who wrote in her small book 'My Own Garden' in 1855:

> *Almost all young people are fond of a garden; and as gardening is fine healthy exercise, it is desirable to encourage a taste for it as much as possible; consequently there are few persons, I believe, who have a family, who if they have any quantity of garden ground themselves, do not set aside a small portion of it for their children.*

Mrs. Loudon continued:

> *Children, however, are often rather badly dealt with in choosing their gardens; for the gardener, if it be left to him, very frequently assigns some portion of the ground, which, either from the natural poverty of the soil, or the badness of the situation, is unfit for any other purpose. This, however, is not right. Children should have their gardens in an open airy situation, with plenty of light and*

> *air; partly because few plants will grow under the drip of trees, and consequently the difficulty of keeping the garden nice is greatly increased, and partly because it is unhealthy for children to work in a garden in a close damp situation.*

Of course I did not read these lines until I acquired a copy of Jane Loudon's little book at a shop in Hay-on-Wye many decades later. And I was content to have an area where I could grow what I liked. Red seemed to be my favourite colour. The oriental poppy excited me when it opened and I found its seed pods exhilarating too. Ideally red flowers should be in a position to catch the evening sun but as I was never at South Muskham in the evenings this did not matter to me. The sheer flamboyance of the scarlet petals and their delicate texture attracted me as I peered into their black centres. Then I begged a red paeony clump of tubers. My grandmother told me that unless she split her large clump in November, when it was dormant, it would sulk and not flower for a year or so. But I was impatient and begged some tubers in the Spring. They duly sulked but flowered the following year. My pyrethrums and grandmother's bonnets (double aquilegia) were all mixed up with annuals such as virginia stock, marigolds (*calendula*) and Eschscholzia (which I could never spell). I remember keeping an empty packet of eschscholzia seeds in my pocket for weeks hoping to impress my friends. But they were more interested in trains and swopping cigarette cards and thought me rather odd to be so interested in gardening.

In these early days I was not very observant but I remember seeing my grandmother come to the back door of the cottage and throw the washing up water over the patch near the pump. The soapy water always seemed to land on a clump of Christmas Roses (*Helleborus niger*) and as the hellebore flourished I realised that soapy water was perhaps good for healthy leaves!

Until after the War my family did not possess a car. But there was a frequent bus service into Newark and I would be put on the bus for home. Quite frequently I had some eggs in a box and a *Charles Ross* apple in my pocket. This was one of a selection of old apples which grew around Jasmine Cottage. I was told that the *Bramley* apple was one of the original distribution by Merryweather's of Southwell in 1876. Years later I was taken to see the original *Bramley* apple tree that had been raised by Betsy Brailsford at Southwell from a seed between 1805 and 1820. It was given an FCC in 1883 and named after the purchaser of Miss Brailsford's cottage, namely a Mr.Bramley.

Apples intrigued me as a young boy. The earliest for eating was *Beauty of Bath* in late July and there always seemed to be several of these apples on the floor. Another early apple was named *Gladstone* (who incidentally was M.P. for Newark in 1832) and this was much sweeter than *Beauty of Bath*. Introduced by Mr. Jackson of Blakedown Nursery near Kidderminster in Worcestershire, it was first called

Jackson's Seedling and in 1883 renamed *Mr. Gladstone.*

Most of the apples grown at Jasmine Cottage were cookers whose names intrigued me. *Peasgood Nonsuch* was a Lincolnshire apple I was told and nearly as good a baking apple as *Bramley*. Along with *Cox's Orange Pippin*, which my grandfather did not grow, it was one of the parents of the *Charles Ross* apple that I coveted regularly. As a fairly large apple that was juicy, sweet and flavoursome, it often prevented me enjoying my teas Another large apple was *Annie Elizabeth*, though the tree never seemed to have many fruits on it.

Rather strangely, I thought, my grandparents grew only the *Conference* pear. They seemed to regard pears as fruits only for connoisseurs and gentry but perhaps it was William Robinson's comment that a pear is only ready to eat on 3 days in the year that put them off. But plums abounded. Once I was delighted to be asked to climb the tall black plum tree called *The Czar* to destroy a magpie's nest. They were pests even in those days.

Early Prolific began the plum season and the greengage usually was the last to ripen. In between came the glorious *Victoria* plums. Some years the sheer weight of fruit would break a branch and they never seemed to have been thinned. The finest of the *Victorias*, however, grew on the front of the cottage. To see large plums growing just below the bedroom window, where I occasionally slept, was incredibly tempting. Downstairs I remember that suckers would sometimes come up through the tiles in a cupboard where the home made gooseberry and damson wines were kept. Damsons of course were a very frequent tree in the hedges around the cottage and I was told that they were originally grown to produce dye.

The potager around my plot grew wonderful vegetables on a rotation basis. One year the potatoes had lovely blue flowers and decades later I wondered whether this was a variety called *Edzell Blue* from Angus in Scotland. Another blue flower that I loved was the globe artichoke (*Cynara scolymus*). As a child I regarded this as a giant thistle. Never a weed was allowed to develop beyond the seedling stage and in the garden shed was a large collection of hoes. 'Knock 'em off!' was the advice I was given regarding weeds and in later years I was known to knock off vegetable seedlings as well!

One Wednesday, coming home early from Mount Primary School, I was prevented from visiting my garden by an incident in Wilson Street near the glorious Parish Church in Newark. At the end of the street I noticed an iron structure which resembled the vaulting horse in the school gym. (I learnt later that this was a fuse box). Coming out of school I was full of energy and took a running jump onto this structure, only to find my left leg firmly wedged between the switch box and the wall. A crowd began to gather and soon an impressive police sergeant arrived and attempted to dislodge me. Having failed to free me he returned to the Police Station in the Market Place and arranged for two Corporation workmen armed with crowbars to move the switch box. The large crowd which by now included the Mayor, the Mayoress, three police officers and a back-up from the Fire Brigade, all applauded. The local newspaper wrote this 'Civic Reception' up at the weekend and on the following Monday morning Miss Moss, my school teacher, took a very dim view of the whole affair. Indeed I felt that I was in danger of being caned. It was a day lost to gardening. No weeds or seedlings were 'knocked off', only a small boy's dignity.

When my grandmother died early in the Second World War (1941) and my grandfather died aged 80 in 1958, I would dearly have liked to buy Jasmine Cottage. It was going for a song but a cantankerous aunt by marriage prevented me. Today the orchard is the site of a bungalow and Jasmine Cottage has been modernised for commuters.

To everyone's surprise I passed the 11-plus examination in 1938 and became a pupil at Magnus Grammar School. Subsequently it was cricket that took the place of gardening each Summer and I would turn out for any village team that would have me. One of these was Edwinstowe and once I remember visiting the Major Oak in Sherwood Forest after scoring only a few runs!

My National Service from 1945 to 1948 did me an enormous amount of good. The rigours of Markeaton Park Training Battalion near Derby earned me the rank of Lance-Corporal! From being in charge of a barrack room of recruits at Lincoln I managed to transfer to the Army Education Corps and eventually play for Northern Command at cricket. After Eaton

Hall O.C.T.U. near Chester I sailed to the Middle East from King George V Dock in Glasgow in the early Autumn of 1947 and ended up as SO2 Education for Gaza Sub-District in Palestine. Here Colonel Napier made me Garden Steward, so even in the Army I was not allowed to escape from plants.

Before leaving Palestine and after the creation of the Jewish State on May 14th 1948, we evacuated to Rafah, on the border with Egypt. Here I shared a tent with Captain Oliver Pottinger (from the Shetlands) and together we organised an expedition down Wadi Musa to Aqaba and then into Jordan. Flash floods had washed away some of the road and we had long detours but eventually we reached Petra. We were the only visiting group on the day. (Today I am told that 600,000 visit each year). Sleeping in the Sinai Desert was a memorable experience and when I came to lecture on Biomes many decades later it was the desert ecosystem of the Sinai that provided many of my illustrations.

Chapter 2: FOUR GARDENS

Following my National Service came four very happy years at Queens' College, Cambridge. Geography was regarded then as a linking subject and a point of view. As such it was a broad education with some considerable depth as well as breadth. In 1948 Queens' was exactly 500 years old and many regard it as the most picturesque college along the Cam.

The gates were looked at 10 p.m. and if undergraduates failed this deadlinc they needed to climb in at several places. On one occasion a group climbed in and as the first undergraduate clambered up the grassy slope under the chestnut trees the emerging moon revealed the profile of the Dean. 'Oh, my God!' exclaimed the student. 'No', came the reply, 'Merely one of His humble servants'. For the chance to display such wit, the Dean let the incident pass.

As Biogeography was one of my main interests I enjoyed the botanic garden along Trumpington Street on regular occasions. The early purple flowering parasitic plant called *Lathraea clandestina* intrigued me and the limestone Rock Garden by the lake had a hollow named a *Doline*. Neither the chronological beds nor the Winter Garden had been created whilst I was up at Cambridge but today they are great didactic features. When visiting my daughter Deborah and her husband Keith (both Dons at Cambridge) I subsequently learnt much about the coloured stems of *Cornus*, *Rubus* and *Salix* and the bark of trees as well as the shrubs which flower in the winter months. Viburnums *farreri, tinus* and *bodnantense 'Dawn'*, various Hamamelis and Cotoneasters, the Mahonias and Jasmine *nudiflorum* and Lonicera x *purpusii* were a delight in the pale winter sunshine.

My own College, though having very picturesque buildings in Old and Cloister Court did not have very good gardens and subsequently the large Cripps Court across the river demolished the Fellows' Garden. I needed to visit Clare, Christ's and Emmanuel Colleges for good gardens.

Whilst still up at Cambridge, following the Tripos, I stayed for an extra year to complete a Postgraduate Certificate in Education and married Patricia (neé Fulton), whom I had met on Field Work in Austria. Subsequently in the Autumn of 1952 I became Geography Master at Baines Grammar School, Poulton-le-Fylde, a few miles inland from Blackpool. We found a small semi-detached house in Hetherington Close, Bispham, with two small garden areas in the front and in the rear. Being rather ignorant of shrubs I chose to fill it with annuals. They seemed to like the sandy soil and high light intensity and were low enough to avoid many of the winds.

But I am afraid that those five years from 1952-57 were very busy indeed and the garden was neglected in the winter. In order to pay the mortgage I needed to augment our income by teaching in the evenings at Blackpool Technical College. As a geographer I taught English to shorthand typists and Current Affairs to Bankers! Each Friday evening I helped run a Youth Club at Poulton-le-Fylde and every Saturday played either hockey for Blackpool or cricket for The Fylde.

Patricia, my wife, was a saint and never grumbled and when Deborah was born in 1953 she would often come along to watch, although we had no car. Philip was born in 1957 which was the year I moved to Hereford to take charge of Geography. I say 'I' because Paddy and the children had to remain in Blackpool for some time while we sold the house in a recession and had major repairs done to the house in Church Road, Tupsley, to the north of Hereford city.

My father had given me a B.S.A. Bantam motor cycle after the 1953 hurricane had ravaged the coast-line of England and Wales. But I still cycled along the Garstang Road the three miles to Poulton each day. It was hard work cycling westwards on some days and all the trees sloped inland.

Eventually in 1958 we were united as a family in Hereford. Only when I sold the Bantam to buy new front gates did I realise how much Deborah had enjoyed riding on the pillion once a week along the country lanes after chapel.

The garden in Hereford was desolate and derelict. It only had one plum tree and Rose *Alberic Barbier* in it and the ground was heavy red marl. I realised that much hard work lay ahead. But it was an opportunity to plan a garden into several compartments – terrace, lawn, vegetable patch, children's play area and so on. As I toiled away I recalled Karel Capek's words –

> .... *clay like lead, squelching and primeval; clay out of which coldness oozes; which bakes in the sun and gets sour in the shade; which yields under the spade like chewing gum; ill tempered, unmalleable, greasy and sticky like Plaster of Paris, slippery like a snake and dry like a brick, unpermeable like tin and heavy like lead.*

The Edwardian house used to be a doctor's home, while its surgery and the lean-to conservatory had been a waiting room. It suggested to me that I might be able to fulfil a long held ambition of growing Lapageria *rosea*, Tibouchina *semidecandra* and even camellias in large pots. In 1957 there were few books to suggest the best camellias to be grown in a cold area and under glass but in 1961 E. B. Anderson published an excellent small took called 'Camellias' (Blandford Press). Additionally, in 1964 Geoffrey Wakefield's 'Camellias for every Garden' (Collingridge) spurred my interest and offered excellent advice on varieties and their culture.

In the year that Adam was born a chance visit to Vincent Square in April 1963 had persuaded me to join in with the inaugural meeting of the International Camellia Society. Here I met such experts as Harold Hillier, Reginald Try, Lionel Fortescue, Leslie Riggall and Charles Puddle. It was Charles who invited me to write a brief account of the first I.C.S. Conference at Lyndhurst in the New Forest in 1964. The Rhododendron and Camellia Yearbook offered articles on 'Camellias in Containers' and visits to such lovely gardens as Borde Hill where the beautiful *Donation* was created from C. japonica *Donckelarii* and C. saluenensis spurred my resolve to grow some of these beautiful evergreens. After *Donation* I grew *Inspiration* because of its neat, dense and upright growth and its deep pink flowers and went on to buy the Les Jury hybrid from New Zealand named *Anticipation*. This proved to be very compact and a cheerful rose-crimson colour. I was advised to grow *E. G. Waterhouse*, which grew like an Irish yew in shape, but its lovely light pink double flowers were short lived and shattered in a few days. On the other hand the stiffly branched and rather open *Leonard Messel* had beautiful apricot and deep pink flowers which lasted much longer. Gradually from Bodnant and from Trehanes Nursery I acquired a small collection of camellias for the garden itself and among these was *Jupiter*, *Donation*, *J. C. Williams*, *Bow Bells*, *Elegans* end the deep red *Nigra* (now *Konron-Koku*).

When we moved to Walsall in 1965 the Head of the Arboretum assured me that it was impossible to grow camellias in the area and I determined to prove him wrong. In a few years time I was amazed that cars would stop outside my small front garden to look at the camellias and magnolias and one even rang my door bell to say thank you! To help with watering I ran a polythene tube from the two downspouts and carried it, perforated, along the top of the soil.

The rear garden had once been an orchard and a few remaining apple and pear trees gave some shade. Soon I had a hedge of camellias *Bow Bells*, *Mary Christian* and *St. Ewe* and elsewhere I grew the higo camellias *Daitairin* and *Furoan* mingled with *C. F. Coates* whose fish-tail leaves never ceased to cause comment from visitors.

In addition to camellias and a few hardy rhododendrons such as *Purple Splendour*, *Sonata*, *Doncaster* and *Yakushimanum*, I became more and more interested in flowering shrubs. After the annuals of Blackpool and the herbaceous perennials of Hereford I became a shrub man. And when I was invited to run courses in 'Plants, personalities and garden styles' at the Extra-Mural Department of Birmingham University in 1972 I began offering lectures to various horticultural societies. Since 1973 the Sutton Coldfield Horticultural Society has invited me to talk to them every year — almost 30 years of pleasure for me!

The move to Areley Kings in 1984 was traumatic. Having taken voluntary redundancy from West Midlands College as a Geography Lecturer I found myself in a small bungalow with a greenhouse. Here I grew the beautiful reticulata camellia *Captain Rawes* which had been introduced from China in

1820. It soon was pushing the roof off and so I offered it to Spetchley Park Garden near Worcester. In exchange I received some tubers of the lovely white paeony moved from Warley Place by Ellen Willmot's sister in the 1930s. Paeony *obovata var alba willmottiana* has lovely white single flowers in early summer and gorgeous seed heads in the autumn and I was happy with the exchange. Other camellias under glass include *Hakurakuten* (or *Wisley White*), *Mrs. D. W. Davis*, *L'Avenire* (also known as *Laurel Leaf*, *Avenire*, *Mary Thomas* and *L'Avvenire*), *Gauntlettii* and its hybrid *Exaltation* (*Gauntlettii* x *Donation*) and the Californians *Guillio Nuccio* and *Bob Hope* (see Illustration 8).

In the front of my small bungalow I have a gravel and conifer garden which I call my 'Sharawadgi'. In Spring it is enlivened by Magnolias *Leonard Messel* and *Stellata*. The aim of making it very labour saving has succeeded and my island bed rear garden (see Illustration 5) also needs the minimum of attention.

The progression, if such it is, from annuals to herbaceous to shrubs and to labour saving planting has given enormous pleasure. There is so much to learn about gardening and so little time to practise it. But I found 'The Hillier Manual of Trees and Shrubs' to be of immense help in choosing shrubs and trees for different soils and situations.

Whilst living in Walsall our three children had brilliant careers at the Universities of Cambridge and Leeds. Deborah became Director of Studies in

Biological Sciences at Newnham College, Cambridge, and has a delightful garden across Midsummer Common at Riverside. Philip and Adam are both very distinguished surgeons at Oxford and Truro respectively. When Philip moves into a house from his large flat in Headington, I am sure that he will enjoy gardening between performing operations at the John Radcliffe Hospital and playing golf. Adam has already won prizes for his vegetables in the Local Show and become very knowledgeable in growing dahlias and rearing rare breeds of poultry. How all my children cope with the multifarious demands of modern life is a miracle. Their success gives me immense satisfaction and pride.

Chapter 3: ALLOTMENTEERING IN THE WEST MIDLANDS.

For eighteen years, from 1965 to 1983, I rented an allotment plot at the Maltshovel site in Walsall. It was owned by a Brewery who persistently tried to evict us so that they could sell the site for housing development. But, with the aid of the National Society of Allotment and Leisure Gardeners, we successfully proved that access was not sufficient for a housing estate to be built between the Ford Brook and the Golf Course and the Maltshovel Cricket Ground.

The Brewery, however, sold the pub and the cricket ground. The pub site became a Motel and the cricket ground disappeared beneath a conglomeration of detached houses. Our rent was raised, of course, from £8 a year for a 30 yard by 10 yard plot to £10 and above and eventually after I left in 1983 the site was indeed sold for houses.

The soil was a heavy Wenlock shale but had the advantage of retaining moisture when improved with compost and manure and leather scraps from the local leather industry. I remember that a fox reared a litter of cubs in this warm pile of leather shavings and subsequently moved to a site beneath my old shed. When it rained and I sat on the old trunk inside the shed I could hear the cubs playing beneath the floor boards.

As the N.S.A.L.G. had temporarily saved our site from development in the 1970s I became interested in the allotment movement in general. Two decades later when I was asked to organise garden tours for New Zealanders I discovered that they were fascinated to learn about the allotment concept and practices. For two centuries allotments have been a minor feature of the English landscape and when Professor Harry Thorpe, a fine geographer, of Birmingham University, was asked to report on allotments to the Government in 1965 he revealed many interesting facts (See Cmnd 4166 H.M.S.O.).

Professor Thorpe suggested that the word 'allotment' bore a stigma and needed to be replaced with a more dignified name. He suggested that the term 'Leisure Gardens' be adopted and that whole families be encouraged to enjoy the plots. All told, Professor Thorpe made 44 major recommendations. None has been officially adopted.

Thus in 1980 there was a good natured protest by allotment holders and Friends of the Earth at the action of the Conservative Government towards land used as allotments. The Secretary of State for the Environment was Michael Heseltine and one of his

Under Secretaries of State was Marcus Fox. Neither were in the least interested that over 120,000 people were on waiting lists for sites in 1980 and the Government withdrew the right of consultation about security of tenure on privately owned land. The Liberal M.P. for the Isle of Wight, Stephen Ross, attempted to persuade the Government to grant more allotment licences on vacant land but gradually this land was appropriated for houses. Ever since Elizabethan times the attitude of Lords and Parliamentarians and the Church generally has been to favour lucrative development rather than allotment of land to deprived tenants of cottages and rented houses.

Indeed in 1845 it was only the fear of a 'peasant revolt' that led to the General Enclosure Act. But this first legal step towards the modern allotment system only resulted in a mere 2,200 acres (or 0.3%) of the 615,000 acres enclosed between 1845 and 1870 to be set aside for allotments.

The 1908 Allotment Act proved fortuitous since the 1914 -18 War highlighted the valuable productiveness of allotments for local food production. Indeed they are the most intensive form of cultivation and the 'Dig for Victory Campaign' during the 1939—45 War resulted in public parks and lawns around the Albert Memorial and at Kew Gardens being ploughed for potato growing. In 1943 the U.S.A. gave 90 tons of vegetable seeds to British allotment holders as seed became scarce in the U.K.

It was in 1930 that the National Society of Allotment and Leisure Gardeners was created and it is called on regularly to give evidence when local authorities covet allotment land for building sites. In Birmingham, adjacent to the Botanic Garden, Guinea Gardens had existed since 1720. These 20-rod plots (600 square yards or twice the size of a standard allotment) once ringed the city and the guinea rent meant that the very poorest could not afford them. But the artisans who could pay made their plots little paradises in the suburbs of Ladywood, Moseley, Handsworth and Aston.

When John Claudius Loudon came to design the Birmingham Botanic Garden in 1831 he noted over 2000 guinea gardens which could then be sold by auction. The summer houses had stoves in them and many garden owners dug wells. But as the city expanded in the mid-nineteenth century the land was sold off for housing. Lord George Calthorpe, however, retained much of the 1840 Malthouse Meadows in Westbourne Road as part of the family Trust. Some plots were sold however and folk like Austin Chamberlain and Joseph Lucas built large houses. The Midland Railway consumed eleven plots.

In 1960 the remaining 80 plots were leased to the City Council and in 1973 Council bulldozers tore up hedges, demolished old summer houses and sheds and removed old fruiting trees. Just why this civic vandalism occurred remains a mystery but thousands of blue engineering bricks and York stone paths were removed. This caused many older gardeners to abandon their plots but under the leadership of

Sheila Hughes and her husband Jeffrey a local Association was formed. Only in 2000 did the Civic Trust respond to a report by David Lambert of the Garden History Society and offer help. The plots now cost £30 a year and the 70 remaining tenants are concerned that when the lease is renewed in March 2002 even the new hedgerow legislation may not save the plots. A fight is inevitable.

In 1985 I moved to a village near Stourport called Areley Kings. Here, in Edwardian times, a benefactor had left some 30 acres for the use of old and young parishioners. There is much hearsay surrounding the allotments and the location of the Will remains a mystery. One senior gardener assures me that the annual rent 'should not exceed the price of a bushel of grain'! In 1963 the rents were four shillings (20p) and by 1985 this had risen to ten shillings (50p). Today the Council maintain the view that the water rates make an annual rent of £8 a bargain. The Acts of 1922 and 1925 authorised Councils to subsidise allotments up to one penny rate but I suspect that few Councils do this.

By the end of the Second World War in 1945 nearly 4000 Societies were affiliated to N.S.A.L.G. but there has been a steady decline since. The peak year was 1914 when according to E. S. Turner (in 'Dear Old Blighty', 1980) some 1.4 million plots produced over 2 million tons of vegetables annually. By 1939 the number of plots had fallen to 815,000 covering 109,000 acres according to Professor Thorpe. Today (in 2002) the number of plots is around the half million mark and a gradual increase in women plot holders is evident.

Professor Thorpe's death in 1977 was a great blow to the allotment movement. His ten principles of Good Design, Beauty, Amenity, Good Maintenance, Productivity, Family use, Community (a pavilion for each site), growing for pleasure, growing for quality and growing for Show are an excellent counsel of perfection which is rarely achieved.

Unlike the Farmer's Union, allotment holders have no clout to negotiate with the Government. And a few horticultural slums masquerading as allotment sites do exist. These allow local Councils to abrogate their responsibility. But other allotments are well run and are aware of J. F. Garner's 'The Law of Allotments' published in 1984 (by Shaw and Sons). This points out that a Council may only take over a site by applying to the Secretary of State and arranging a public enquiry with a Government Inspector in attendance. Even so the huge boom in land and house prices (a 14% rise in 2001) makes the future of some allotment sites problematical.

As an escape from the pressures of life, as a chance of meeting others from many walks of life, as a valuable source of fresh fruit, flowers and vegetables, and as a welcome form of leisure activity, I have found an allotment a very valued place to cultivate. Sadly many young and middle-aged people today shy away from the necessary regular attention that an allotment requires. Their priorities lie elsewhere, their income has increased greatly, they prefer to take their family in the car to the seaside and they would rather watch a football match on T.V. than dig at the allotment. To keep in touch with the land is, I feel a valuable part of living and for people from many walks of life to co-operatively produce food and flowers is an important component of community life.

I like to hear Wesley Jones say "Would never 'ave rasps. They 'arbours a lot of rubbish", even though I grow several rows of *Autumn Bliss* raspberries and deep freeze them for winter use. I remember one plot holder saying of a very lazy neighbour "He's here today — the pub must be closed". And I recall Eddie (sometimes called The Sheriff) saying as I rode my bicycle down the path "Watch out, me bloody marrow's moving"! Of the 80 plots at Areley Kings (see Illustration 9), perhaps a fifth are not cultivated at present. On the adjacent field Willed for the use of parishioners, there are plans to build a new village hall. "Will the allotments survive this development?" is a comment I hear very frequently.

Chapter 4:
TRAVELS IN THE TROPICAL WORLD

In order to lecture on 'Modern World Problems' and the 'Economic Development of Selected Tropical Countries' I needed to make study visits abroad at regular intervals. The Commonwealth Institute in Kensington High Street were an invaluable help in recommending Colleges and Universities as accommodation from 1969 onwards. In that year a Field Study Group visited India and Sri Lanka in July and August. I remember studying water supply around Madras, vegetable production centred on the Lal Bagh gardens of Bangalore, eucalypts at Ootacamund and tea production near Nuwara Eliya in Sri Lanka.

It then occurred to me that I ought to find out about the Lake Volta scheme in Ghana. Kwame Nkrumah had declared independence in 1957 and expected the Akosombo Dam near Accra to produce electricity for the Tema industrial complex. The large lake which stretched inland for some 240 miles would inevitably affect the country's economy and transport system and I was keen to see at first hand some of the effects. Here I had the good fortune to know Rev. William Whittle who, with his wife Grace, had gone out to the Gold Coast to minister at Wenchi. From Takoradi they had walked for eleven days in 1921 to reach Wenchi and had, as their house boy, Kofi Busia, the eight year old son of an Ashanti chief. When Nkrumah was deposed in 1970 Kofi Busia became Prime Minister and arranged for the Whittle's to re-visit Ghana as his guests. In his Presidential jet the journey which had taken them eleven days in 1921 only took 25 minutes in 1971. The pace of change has changed.

I was introduced to the Prime Minister at The Castle, Accra, and his Letters of Introduction enabled me to stay very comfortably at Cape Coast University and inland at Kumasi and Bolgatanga. It was fascinating to learn about cocoa production and to research the methods being tried to produce better millet and cotton crops. I recall with sadness how foreign debts compelled Kofi Busia to devalue the cedi in January 1972 by 44% and this was a contributory factor to his overthrow by Colonel Acheampong and other subsequent military leaders.

So many incidents spring to mind about this Christmas visit to Ghana but two are especially vivid. I remember being woken at night by a loud crack and at daylight I saw that the dry Harmattan wind had caused a long wooden table to split down the middle. And that day we were taken out in a surf boat and experienced the way in which ships were unloaded before the ports of Takoradi and Tema were constructed. The surf is very impressive all along the Ghanaian coast.

Equally vivid was my stay at Piarco University on Trinidad island and the visit to the neighbouring island of Tobago in the Caribbean. As I queued up for lunch one day at Piarco the man behind me explained that he had chosen Trinidad to retire to from New York because 'here one can be poor with dignity'. I fear that Port of Spain is a less peaceful place to be poor in today. I studied tourism in the Caribbean and marvelled how little it helped ordinary people in those days. The multinationals benefited most and agriculture was often deprived of labour at critical times by the demands of large hotels for casual labour.

Prom Trinidad I flew to Georgetown in Guyana and with incredible good fortune I was given hospitality by Walter and Elma Fraser. Wattie, who owned an emporium in Regent Street, Georgetown, had once been Minister of Finance in the Government. His help in transporting me around and enabling me to study cattle rearing on the Rupununi savannahs and to experience something of the Amazon Rain Forest ecosystem was invaluable. Without Wattie's telephone calls I could not possibly have crowded so many experiences into the few weeks I was in Guyana in 1975. Wattie arranged for the Bookers Company to fly me around over the cane fields and the white sands area where bauxite was obtained. He also made it possible for me to visit the unforgettable Kaieteur Falls on the Potaro River near Mount Roraima. Each Sunday a small plane flew twenty people to the Orinduick Falls and the Kaieteur Falls for the day and the thrill of seeing this 1000 foot waterfall will always remain in my mind. So will the sight of the *Victoria Regia* water lily first discovered by Schomburgk on the river Berbice on January 1st 1837. In his 1840 'History of the Vegetable Kingdom' William Rhind records how Haenke discovered this great water lily soon after Schomburgk and

> *on descrying it, the botanist fell on his knees and gave utterance to his religious and scientific enthusiasm in passionate exclamations of adoration towards the Creator, improvising a Te Deum.*

Fortunately for my companion guide I never trained as a singer!

Of course I always visited botanic gardens wherever I travelled and after a World Tour was able to offer a Course entitled 'Gardens of Empire'. This included my travels in the footsteps of Joseph Dalton Hooker in Assam, Sikkim and Nepal. En route to the Sigalila ridge, which is so frequently visited today, I stayed in Darjeeling. On Easter Day, 1998 the view of the rising sun colouring the snows of Kanchenjunga was magical. Equally captivating was the view from Kyllong Rock in Assam en route to Cherrapunji. To compare Hooker's description in his Himalayan Journal with the degraded view today was sad. Much forest is destroyed to grow potatoes.

One of the few remaining shangri-las is surely Lake Toba in Northern Sumatra. The small botanic garden nearby boasted a *Rafflesia* I was told but I failed to see the huge red flower. And likewise at the very fine Bogor garden inland from Jakarta on Java I was too late to see this amazing parasitic flower named after the famous Charles Raffles. But I saw hundreds of species orchids both at Bogor and again at the Botanic Garden in the centre of Bali.

The hybrid orchids of Singapore are legendary and very well known today, and from Singapore I went on to Melbourne in Australia and to New Zealand. Most of the botanic gardens in New Zealand (Christchurch, Dunedin and Wellington) were founded in the 1860s. After that time nearly all the native flora was destroyed and grasses imported to create sheep pastures. But on the eastern outskirts of Wellington Job Wilton retained an area of native vegetation. This rare remnant of New Zealand's flora at Otari is an invaluable insight into the native species and their use in gardens today.

Subsequent visits abroad included South Africa where the Fynbos vegetation demonstrated at the Kirstenbosch on the slopes of Table Mountain is so fascinating. The proteas, the leucodendrons, the leucospermums (like brightly coloured pin cushions), the ericas, the strelitzias and cycads are full of interest.

Among the various gardens visited in South Africa were Freshwoods at Elgin, Old Nectar at Jonkerschaek, Hortus Botanicus at Stellenbosch, and Cellars at Hottentot, but the most beautiful is at Kloof, 12 miles inland from Durban. Here Leslie

Riggall has created a wonderful 35-acre garden called Fern Valley where he can pick an orchid and a camellia on every day of the year. Here is the only place outside of Japan where everyone of Wilson's 50 Kirume Azaleas are grown. Here, at the age of 90, Leslie Riggal remains very active. He has left the garden, with an endowment, to the State so that it will remain in perpetuity as one of the finest gardens in the world.

Beauty spiced with wonder is the lure of travel and I hope to share the knowledge gained with audiences and classes for many years to come.

Chapter 5: RESEARCH INTO LANDSCAPE PARKS ALONG THE TRENT VALLEY IN STAFFORDSHIRE

In 1982 it was suggested to me that a Research Degree would be a good idea. Whenever I met garden historians I seemed to spend much time in defending Capability Brown and so it seemed appropriate to investigate his contribution to the landscape parks and gardens along the Trent Valley in Staffordshire. One misguided garden historian dismissed Brown as a 'mercenary minimalist' and this ignorant remark needed refuting. Thus I enrolled at Birmingham University as a Postgraduate and travelled to Stafford Record Office and the William Salt Library every working day for a year. Lord Harrowby also allowed me to spend a month of weekdays in his muniment rooms at Sandon Hall. He was a fine and benevolent estate owner.

I decided that the century 1750 to 1850 would be a good time scale and studied in chronological order Shugborough, Ingestre, Trentham, Fisherwick, Tixall, Keele, Beaudesert, Sandon, Blithefield, Swynnerton and Teddesley landscape parks and gardens. I argued that whilst social, political and aesthetic factors played an important role in the creation of designed landscapes in eighteenth century Staffordshire, most emparkers were more influenced by a hard-headed economic approach than by either literary or visual stimuli.

Secondly, I discovered that, although Lancelot Brown (1716-1783) was commissioned to prepare plans for four of the eleven parks and whilst his activity in the County was inspirationally paramount, yet his operational role as a practitioner was overshadowed in quantity by the work of William Emes (1730-1803).

Most people think of the Potteries or the Black Country when the word 'Staffordshire' is mentioned, but along the middle Trent Valley south of Trentham the landscape is predominantly rural and still owes much of its character to the parks created in the eighteenth century.

At an auction in Knole I managed to acquire a copy of Dr. Plot's 'Natural History of Staffordshire'. This 1686 volume has illustrations by Michael Burgher which show much of the formal gardens which surrounded country houses in the seventeenth century. For Trentham uniquely in the county, there is a wealth of cartographic evidence for the 17th century formal avenues, canals and parterres near the house. The Leveson-Gowers then asked Capability Brown in 1759 to produce a fine plan with the river Trent dammed to form a lake and the house rebuilt. Earlier Brown had produced plans for Swynnerton (c.

1756?) and for Ingestre (definitely 1756). A plan by William Emes in 1769 for Keele prompted me to write an article for 'Country Life' on the work of Emes in Staffordshire. And the 'Geographical Magazine' printed my article on 'The Ephemeral Fisherwick Park' in June, 1982.

Brown had designed and planted Fisherwick Park for the Earl of Donegal between 1776 and 1779 and built a magnificent Palladian mansion set in extensive grounds five kilometres east of Lichfield. The six water-colours which John Spyers made in 1786 of Fisherwick show its great merit. My article described the sale of 1808 and the felling of almost all the 100,000 trees that Brown had planted. Recently in 1963 gravel exploitation was started by B.C.A. The district council had refused this application but the Minister of Housing and Local Government allowed the exploitation to begin and the park to be destroyed.

It would be tedious to describe in any detail the findings of my 1983 Thesis and copies are lodged both at Birmingham University and at the William Salt Library in Stafford. But it is fascinating to enter the world of the eighteenth century *cognoscenti* and see how their estates were affected by pollution in the case of Trentham and gambling debts in the case of Shugborough. Tixall was amalgamated with Ingestre which now embalms part of the park in a golf course.

The estate at Keele is a University Campus after the Edwardian extravagances of Ralph Sneyd

(1863-1949) which included racehorses, yachting and shooting, led him into debt and exile in Wiltshire. The lack of an heir from his three marriages was perhaps an additional factor which led to the rapid decline of the Keele estate. Then double death duties led to the sale of 1,784 hectares for the campus of the University of Keele.

Beaudesert was the subject of one of Humphry Repton's 'Red Books' in 1814 and his water colours show the fine Elizabethan Hall on the eastern flanks of Cannock Chase. But the Pagets were far more interested in Plas Newyd on Anglesey and both mounting debt and agricultural depression resulted in the sale of much timber around Beaudesert. At the end of the nineteenth century revenues from the Chase coalfields declined and, as expenses associated with Beaudesert as a busy sporting estate mounted, and as the fire in the west wing in 1909 involved further expense, Beaudesert became increasingly deserted. It was offered for sale in 1924 and in between 1932 and 1935 the fine four-storeyed Hall was demolished. The 1963 aerial photograph showed that the old Deer Park was now covered with conifers. Around Castle Ring and between Cuckoo Bower and William Emes' old kitchen garden, Scout and Guide camps are clearly visible. Rhododendron *ponticum* has spread and only a very small fragment of the medieval Great Hall survives amid the old hollow sweet chestnuts.

Sandon Hall, however, is still maintained by the Harrowby family. The sixth Earl died in May 1987 aged 94. From 1770 to the present time the enterprise and benevolence of the Harrowbys has been chronicled in the landscaping of the inner and outer parks. Samuel Wyatt's farm still graces the Dale and the transcripts of the conversations between Nathaniel Ryder, the first Lord Harrowby, and William Emes between 1778 and 1787 are now available. The diaries were translated into longhand between 1949 and 1966 by Mr. Kenneth Perrin of Great Comberton in Worcestershire on the initiative of the Sixth Earl. Like all the Harrowbys, he was an 'Earl of Creation' with a prophetic eye of taste and had a caring relationship with his tenants and visitors. He would arrange for excursion trains to bring visitors to Sandon from the Potteries and ensure their enjoyment on his land up to the outbreak of the Second World War.

Of the other Staffordshire estates, Blithefield now belongs to the South Staffordshire Company and a 320-hectare reservoir dominates the landscape. Swynnerton, once the seat of the Fitzherbert family, remains in private hands. The kitchen garden which appears on Brown's plan is now a housing estate. Some of his shrubbery which, as in many of his plans, was planted with flowering shrubs and trees still exists.

Teddesley Hall was built by Edward Lyttelton from the proceeds of a hoard of coins found behind some panels at Pillaton Hall. The Lytteltons took a keen first hand interest in their estates and in farming methods in the Napoleonic Wars and throughout the Victorian era. Few Staffordshire landowners were as friendly with their tenants as the

Lytteltons and such fraternisation offended General Dyott of Freeford Hall, near Lichfield. As a result, Dyott refused to join Lord Lyttelton at the Lichfield Agricultural Dinner in 1824, saying

> *.........the mingling of rank in society in the familiar situation of a tavern table is incompatible with the order necessary to preserve rank and dignity of station.*

The Lytteltons became Lord Hathertons and Edward Richard (1815-1888) became Liberal M.P. for Walsall and South Staffordshire from 1846 to 1852. But the third Baron wrote in his Diary in 1897 'Oh what a dreadful thing it is to inherit a debt'. Thus land in Walsall was sold for building on and the Arboretum came into existence when limestone workings ended. The Hall was demolished after the Second World War and, as elsewhere, many tenants purchased their farms at very reasonable prices.

Shugborough illustrates the transition from a park ornamented with classical buildings to a model farm and then a deserted estate in the mid-19th century. The Anson line ended in 1773 but Thomas Anson's sister Janette had married Sambrook Adams. It was their son George Adams (1731-1789) who changed his name to Anson in 1773 and took over the Shugborough estates. It was his son who became Viscount Anson in 1806 and who transformed the ornamental park into a model farm. The great flood of 1795 had swept away the Pagoda over the Sherbrook and the ruins near the house. Afterwards the lake in the park was drained and to the east of the Tower of the Winds a large walled kitchen garden was created. The villagers who once lived in the park had been rehoused in Great Haywood and the main Stafford-Rugeley road was diverted out of the park, through a glacial overflow channel in the Satnall Hills. The land to allow this new road to be built was purchased from Lord Uxbridge of Beaudesert in 1803. Also a new channel for the River Sow was dug and Mr. Webb was commissioned to create a metal bridge near the Chinese pavilion.

As a successful farmer, Anson persuaded Wyatt to convert the base of the 'Tower of the Winds' into a dairy and Wedgwood of Etruria supplied pots. In J. C. Loudon's 1826 'Gardener's Magazine' the gardener Andrew Johnston of Shugborough records growing a pineapple weighing 5.7 kgs.

However the gambling debts incurred by Viscount Anson in 1826 amounted to £330,000; yet he continued to gamble for high stakes. Thus the contents of the Hall were sold in 1842 along with the contents of 15, St. James Square. The main Euston to Scotland railway line was allowed to run through the park in 1847 to raise money. But debts were still £700,000 and Shugborough was deserted until the mortgage of 1854. Then the cheapest furniture available was bought to refurnish the Hall. This was Louis XV1 furniture and French boule clocks and fine china.

In 1960 the fourth Earl died and Shugborough was transferred to the Treasury. Because of the

Staffordshire County Council's enlightened policy in leasing Shugborough, the National Trust have been able to look after the Hall despite the lack of any endowment from the Anson family. The 18th century stables are a fine museum, the farm educates children in animal welfare and the present Anson family is allowed to occupy 17 rooms in the Hall. They are very fortunate indeed, in view of their troubled family history.

These are just a few of the facts which emerge from my thesis. Since 1880 over 30 Staffordshire mansions have been demolished and their gardens allowed to become overgrown. There are of course other landscape parks in Staffordshire which thrive, including Chillington, Enville, Himley, Patshull and Weston. All have been variously connected with Lancelot Brown. I shall continue to be an advocate of Brown's genius, not only as the finest landscape gardener of the eighteenth century, but also as an all round gardener who created many fine shrubberies full of flowering shrubs and trees. These compensated for the labour-intensive formal parterres that he was asked to remove and which could easily be recreated in a few years, if so desired. Evidence of this can be seen at Blenheim where Ms. Duchêne recreated the Italianate water gardens in a few years between 1927 and 1930.

Illustration 2: A corner of a Birmingham Garden called 'Candlesticks' — a model garden

A superb town garden which flourished from 1958 to 1978 at 16 Heaton Drive, Edgbaston, Birmingham

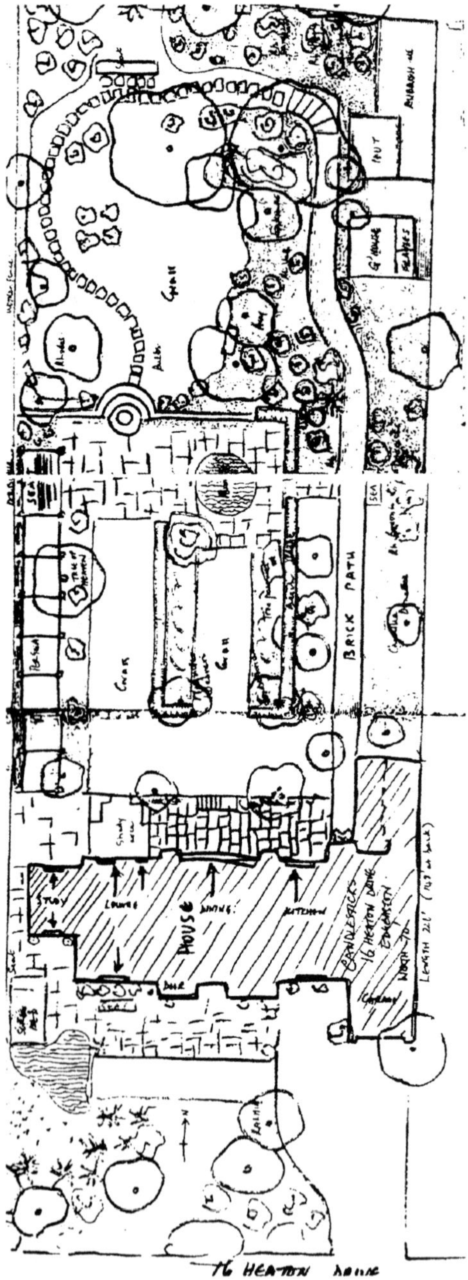

Area =
one third of an acre

(226 ft × 70 ft)

Illustration 3: Plan of 'Candlesticks'

Illustration 4: The Pin Mill at Bodnant in North Wales
— my favourite garden

Illustration 5:
A corner of the author's Worcestershire garden, with
Cyclamen sculpture by John Tonks F.R.B.S.

Illustration 6: part of a potager

Illustration 7: Steps as a focal point in an urban garden

Illustration 8: Camellias — (clockwise) *Hakurakuten (= Wisley White), Debbie, Guillio Nuccio, l'Avenire, Mrs D. W. Davis*

Illustration 9: The author's Areley Kings Allotment

Chapter 6: LECTURING ON PLANTS, PERSONALITIES AND GARDEN STYLES AT HOME AND ABROAD

That the Sutton Coldfield Horticultural Society have invited me to talk to them every year since 1973 delights and amazes me. I enjoy lecturing immensely and Mary Cummings in the Southampton Press of New York wrote:

> *Walter Wilde is a speaker who hits the ground running and picks up steam as he goes. Fuelled by an obvious passion for his subject and blessed with the incredible multi-octave intonational range of the uninhibited Brit, Mr. Wilde could easily captivate an audience with no knowledge of English at all.*

I blush with pleasure!

It is essential, of course, to know your subject well enough to be able to dispense with notes. You then have direct contact with your audience, especially if you are able, as I am, to dispense with the microphone and fill the hall with well- modulated speech and with enthusiasm. Moreover the talk and the presentation of slides must be well structured. The slides themselves need to be of the finest quality today and just the right number presented to make the lecture memorable and enjoyable. As Seneca said, the object is to 'Instruct, Delight and Move' and not to go on for too long.

Of course, taking University classes requires a different technique, as handouts and the interplay of ideas come into it. And it is advisable to arrange Field Visits. For, as Avray Tipping wrote of Bodnant:

> *It is a garden to visit and is realisable only by direct vision. The interest is too large and the beauty too delicate and intimate for photography.*

Indeed in many modem gardening books the photographs are downright misleading as to the design of the garden and its vistas. The overuse of telephoto lenses is to blame.

My courses at Birmingham were initially on a broad canvas. One benevolent colleague called the approach 'heroic'! But gradually the courses on 'The English Landscape Garden', 'Victorian Gardens',' Edwardian Gardens' and 'Modern Gardens' etc. were offered with greater depth and experience. Gardens associated with little known garden designers such as William Emes, Norah Lindsay and Percy Cane were studied in depth. And long before the Gertrude Jekyll cult was revived in the 1980s we were studying her collaboration with Edwin Lutyens and the gardens they designed. We studied personalities such as Marianne North and her paintings at Kew. We analysed the college gardens of Cambridge and Oxford and we studied both Twentieth Century Men and Women Gardeners. As a result of wide travels in the Tropical World it was possible also for me to offer a 'Gardens of Empire' Course which studied over a score of gardens associated with the British, French and Dutch Empires.. A lecture tour of New Zealand allowed me to offer a course on antipodean gardens.

Additionally both the Workers Educational Association at Wolverhampton and the 'Gateway' centre in Shrewsbury commissioned me to offer a variety of Courses in garden styles. This was before the Shropshire County Council reduced my remuneration to a ridiculously low figure. Attendance figures at my Courses have always been about 30 and I am pleased that the University has always made money from me.

Winterbourne, in Edgbaston Park Road, Birmingham, was the centre for my Courses from 1972 to 2002. The house and garden had been created by John and Margaret Nettlefold in Edwardian times and were a superb setting for garden orientated courses. Today it is the School for Business Studies and only a few botanical courses are run there.

Fortunately I have been able to extend my lecturing both to New York and to New Zealand. In 1989 it was Rosemary Verey, in her garden at Barnsley House, near Cirencester, who encouraged me to try for an American lecture tour, She suggested the Brooklyn Botanic Garden, Longwood Gardens, Wave Hill, the Hamptons and Philadelphia and supplied me with contacts. Of these Bill Shank, the founder of the Horticultural Alliance of the Hamptons, was adventurous enough to invite me to talk at Bridgehampton on October 21st 1991. The President, Elizabeth Lear, wrote after my talk

> *Your lecture was fantastic. I just want to thank you for sharing your knowledge, experience, delightful sense of humour and bountiful energies with us.*

In 1993 I enjoyed giving further lectures in New York on 'Edwardian Gardens' and on 'Capability Brown', both to the Horticultural Alliance of the Hamptons and at the Grolier Club where the Royal Oak Foundation meet. The following year allowed me to take part in a Landscape Day at The Parrish Art Museum, Jobs Lane, Southampton, New York. Virgin Atlantic flew me first class on this enjoyable occasion. Subsequently I have travelled regularly to New York to lecture to various Societies and enjoyed the experience enormously. Travelling around the Hamptons and viewing gardens that need to come alive for May 23rd when many New Yorkers come to the Hamptons has been an education and a pleasure. It is said that there are more landscape designers in the Hamptons than in any other comparable area on earth. They are doing battle with the increasing threat from deer in the pine trees. Apparently the only plants that deer dislike are alliums, daffodils and day lilies. I look forward to returning to lecture in the Hamptons in 2002, and to enjoying the delightful garden created by the Shanks in Amagansett. It is a 'him' and 'hers' garden as Bill likes formality and Erika prefers swathes of mixed herbaceous and shrubs.

Lecturing in New Zealand is a totally different experience. The Marlborough Garden Festival takes place in the north-east of South Island and flying in from Wellington across Cook Strait reveals huge areas of vines and olives. The Hunter wine making family sponsor the Festival each November and Marlborough comes alive. I fitted in this event as part of a Lecture Tour for various Charities. This included the excellent new garden complex at Hamilton to the south of Auckland, the art decor area near Napier and the Race Course at Wellington. This latter lecture enabled an organisation, wonderfully led by Adrienne Manthel, to buy land for handicapped children to ride horses on. After Wellington and Marlborough came the Rose Society at Nelson where Pam and Jerry Goulter gave wonderful hospitality on their sheep farm in 88 Valley. Flying down to Invercargill in the very south, along the foothills of the Southern Alps was a memorable experience. And subsequently I lectured in a marquee at Cheviot in aid of a new cricket pavilion on the famous ground there. Roger and Ian Macfarlane were wonderful hosts and I noticed that Roger had scored over five centuries for the Cheviot cricket team in previous years. Near Invercargill my generous hosts were Joyce and John Robins and the rate of growth in their new garden amazed me.

On this tour my last lecture was given in Rangiora to be north of Christchurch and subsequently it was a joy to drive into Arthur's Pass and see fields of wild lupins and the beautiful alpine buttercup (Ranunculus *lyallii*) on the Dawson's trail. So much of New Zealand's native flora has been destroyed in the interests of sheep that the Arthur's Pass area deserves special protective action.

Very soon after I left New Zealand in 1959, Barbara Lea Taylor was asked to write a 'Portrait of a peripatetic gardener' for the New Zealand Gardener Magazine. Amusingly it was printed as follows:

> *It's hard to classify Walter Wilde. I suppose you could say he's a man of many parts which would probably make him fall about laughing since he's well endowed with a sense of humour. World traveller, international lecturer, gardener and garden writer are the labels that immediately come to mind. He was born and still lives in England and he read geography at Queens' College, Cambridge, the same college where Erasmus wrote in 1509*
>
> *"A garden is a place dedicated to the honourable pleasures of rejoicing the eye, refreshing the nose and renewing the spirit".*
>
> *He taught in grammar schools for fourteen years before completing a Research Degree in Designed Landscapes and*

branching into lecturing in Continuing Studies for Adults at Birmingham University.

In the long university vacation, he takes groups of people on tours of Britain's most beautiful gardens and goes on lecture tours overseas.

Almost every year he meets a party of New Zealand garden lovers, organised by local rosarian Sally Allison, and for ten days he guides them through the gardens and great houses of a particular area of the British Isles, imparting generous dollops of garden history and anecdotes along the way.

America loves his witty and flamboyant lecturing style. In his brochure he lists thirty-seven subjects ranging from 'Gardens down the Centuries' to 'Travels in the Amazon Rain Forest' and he gets rave, although somewhat ambiguous, reviews.

The Southampton Press of New York writes: 'Walter Wilde is a speaker who hits the ground running and picks up steam as he goes. Fuelled by an obvious passion for his subject and blessed with the incredible multi-octave intonational range of the uninhibited Brit, Mr. Wilde could easily captivate an audience with no knowledge of English at all'.

But at heart Walter is a serious academic with a love of literature, cricket and music, although the last passion does make him burst into song rather often.

When I caught up with him last November at Hunter's Garden Marlborough where he spoke on 'The Garden Evolution,' he had already completed a lecture tour of Long Island, New York, trekked the Himalayas, and guided a group of New Zealand enthusiasts around the gardens of Ireland. He had also lost all his clothes somewhere in the Canadian Rockies — misdirected luggage I think — which had meant a new basic wardrobe.

"I am very much interested in garden styles", he said. "When I was doing sixth form English literature, I had three books to study — Milton's 'Paradise Lost' for its wonderful prose, Shakespeare's 'Twelfth Night' as an introduction to formal gardens and the countryside and Bacon's Essays, 1625. The first essay was 'Truth' but I always flicked over to the essay on gardens."

Walter used the following wise and clever quote from Francis Bacon to preface his Garden Marlborough lecture:

"God Almighty first planted a garden and indeed it is the purest of human pleasures. It is the greatest refreshment to the spirits of man, without which buildings and palaces are but gross handiworks.

And a man shall ever see that when ages grow to civility and elegancy, men come to build stately sooner than to garden finely —as if gardening were the greater perfection".

"Gardening is a fine art", he says. "You have a brick — and a brick is a brick and remains so — but you buy a shrub and it changes. People create their own personal paradise which can alter with age."

His favourite plants are camellias, dwarf rhododendrons, maples and "some" roses. He lists them — R. moyesii Geranium R. cantabrigiensis, Constance Spry, Graham Thomas, Gertrude Jekyll and Shropshire Lass — a bunch for a connoisseur.

"If I could have just one garden it would be Bodnant in North Wales. I take a group there nearly every year", he says. But he visited our Akaroa gardens before he flew away. In fact he spent a pleasant morning weeding and deadheading in one of them and was so enchanted by its romantic charms that he vowed he'd be back. Can the antipodean delights of Banks Peninsula compete with the call of the Conway Valley?

Recently I was invited to make a return visit as a lecturer to the Bewdley Festival in Worcestershire in 2002. After the previous year's sell-out, I requested an increased fee. The organiser replied, "Oh no! You are only local." A prophet is not without honour except in his own County! (sic). It is only fair to add that the Bewdley Committee <u>did</u> increase my fee somewhat for October, 2002 and the organiser pointed out that there would not be any jet lag as I travelled the few miles along the Severn between Areley King's and Bewdley!

Chapter 7:
A MODEL GARDEN IN THE CENTRE OF BIRMINGHAM

Of all the fine gardens in Edgbaston that I have been asked to analyse none impressed me more than 'Candlesticks' at 16, Heaton Drive off Augusta Road and adjacent to the Eagle Star Insurance building on the Hagley Road. It was created by Mr. Siviter Smith, a Birmingham solicitor, between 1956 and 1965 and was begun well before the house was built. This third of an acre garden is well worth chronicling because of the immense care and wise principles which went into its creation and because of its subsequent demise.

Mr. Siviter Smith was a patient man who took three years to create his oasis of delight. His planning was meticulous and comprehensive. Realising that a town garden had to be inward looking, he created internal eye-catchers and foci. The original site was a field full of brambles, an old hedgerow, dead trees, the base of a wall and tall weeds. This was akin to the state of Sissinghurst when the Nicolsons moved in around 1932 but on a much smaller scale.

The climate of Edgbaston affords a late spring and an early autumn compared with the south and west of England. Temperatures are lower because the site is almost 600 feet up and the strength the of the sun is reduced by the urban atmosphere. The micro-climate of Heaton Drive is much harsher than that of the Botanical Gardens which are only a quarter of a mile away. And as more and more trees are lopped in the area the micro-climate becomes less favourable for many plants. Moreover, the sandy acidic soil dries out quickly and requires irrigation in summer. It is also a hungry soil which needs bonemeal and compost every autumn for best results.

Because restlessness is a feature everywhere today this garden was designed as a restful retreat which offers peace and pleasure (see Illustration 3). The buildings, such as a greenhouse and the shed, were made of cedar which mellowed to an unobtrusive grey and which harmonised with the garden as a whole. The paving was York stone but the walls were of local Gornal stone which weathered to a soft honey colour. Places where the sun and where the shade could be enjoyed were planned. The pools were of a circular design and when it rains the patterns in the pool may be enjoyed from sheltered seats.

The overall factor in design was to create firmness with informality. The informal and free planting softens the severe outlines of paths and low walls and steps in the rear garden. At the front the sun terrace overlooks a wonderfully eclectic planting of flowering shrubs, herbaceous, bulbs and small trees which were planned to be viewed from the house. When Convolvulus appeared amid a patch of Euphorbias the whole area was excavated and a shallow pebble pool created for the birds to bathe in.

The excavated material produced a raised alpine bed at eye level as one turned to go round the side of the house towards the pergola.

The whole garden was deliberately over planted and pruning was necessary from time to time. Ground cover plants (such as those advocated by Margery Fish at East Lambrook Manor) reduced the appearance of weeds. Indeed the heavily planted front garden of the Siviters took far less labour and time than the neighbouring lawns.

This garden layout was approached with three special requirements. Firstly it had to look really interesting all the year round and not only in the summer months. Secondly, because of the unfavourable climate, it had to appear interesting from every room in the house as well as from within the garden itself. And thirdly the house and garden had to harmonise and not appear as separate entities.

In order to achieve these requirements a number of rules were followed. About sixty percent of the plants needed to be evergreen. Only fairly permanent and perennial plants were used, mostly shrubs and bulbs. And the flowering or period of foliage colour of the plants had to be evenly spread. A quarter would be spring flowering, a quarter would flower in June and July, a quarter would look good in the autumn and the last quarter would flower in the winter period from November to March.

Each window from the house had its own vista. From the study the view was along the substantial pergola with its many clematis and climbing roses, schizandra, tropaeolum, eccremocarpus, hydrangeas, ivies and so on. From the French windows of the drawing room the view was between the beech hedges, over the circular steps, across the bulbs area in grass to the wall niche with its yuccas and seated area (see Illustration 2). From the wide Dining Room window the view was past a border of trees such as the Embothrium *Norquinco* and plants such as tree paeonies, across the circular pool to the small woodland glade. From the kitchen window the view proceeded up the garden path, past a potager to an iron seat amid rhododendrons *Doncaster, Cynthia* and *Yakushimanum* to the wall buttresses. All this was looking to the North so that the sun was mostly behind the viewer in the house. The house is predominantly brick with some wood and looks 'at one with the garden' both in the sunny front and shady back areas.

In the rear, cross vistas were arranged where possible. At the top of the pergola for example a seat looked across the pool and through an arch in the beech hedge to a seat amid the rhododendrons. And a sycamore tree which was mature and on the site was deliberately left to reduce the impact of the tall Eagle Star building beyond the tall garden wall.

In general the Siviter Smiths preferred soft rather than vivid colours except in early spring when they had been starved of colour during the winter months. Thus no annuals were used in this garden although near the house some pelargoniums were allowed. Nor were dahlias or chrysanthemums used.

Instead the subtle shades and shapes of leaves were preferred.

As no-one can be quite sure what a garden will look like in twenty years the Siviter Smiths were quite prepared to thin out shrubs when necessary. The only insecticides used in this garden were the ones entirely harmless to birds and humans, namely Derris, Pyrethrin and Rotenone.

To my knowledge the only printed remarks on this garden appeared in a short article written by Mr. Siviter Smith for the RHS Journal. It listed the Rhododendrons that he grew at 'Candlesticks' and these included *Yakushimanum, Sonata, Purple Splendour, Damozel, Wardii, Neriiflorum, Bo-Peep, Strigellosum, Tally Ho, Lady Chamberlain Gleam, Humming Bird, Glaucophyllum* and *Polar Bear.* This last named fragrant white rhododendron which flowers in August, reached a height of 8 feet before opening any flower buds. All told, it was a collection for a connoisseur.

Some time after Mr. Siviter Smith's death his widow found the upkeep of this garden too demanding. After the sale the plants in the front garden were removed in a skip by the new owner to make way for a semicircular driveway. I was told by a neighbour's gardener that most of the rear garden had been made into a playground for the new owner's children. But for over twenty years this was the finest city garden imaginable and I was privileged to enjoy it, and learn from it.

Chapter 8:
MY TOP TEN GARDENS

Over a period of thirty years it has been my recurring pleasure to arrange visits to very many gardens for my University classes and in preparation for my lectures. Occasionally I am asked for my top ten gardens and this poses a problem. How do you judge a top class garden?

For me it must have good plants and possess a unity of design. To avoid any invidious argument about ranking I have placed my top ten gardens in alphabetical order. They are:— Bodnant, Crathes, Edzell, Fern Valley, Mount Congreve, Powis, Preen Manor, Sutton Place, Stourhead and the Valley Gardens in Windsor Great Park.

Bodnant

With such a superlative site on the eastern bank of the River Conway and overlooking the Snowdon range of mountains, Bodnant is a most attractive garden. The eighty acres open to the public by the National Trust has very eclectic and well manicured plantings (see Illustration 4).

When F. C. Puddle became Head Gardener in 1921 the Aberconways had been in residence since 1874 and had planted the Hiraethlyn Dell with numerous conifers, magnolias and rhododendrons. In Edwardian times Mr. Henry Pochin's daughter Laura had persuaded her son to create a series of terraces below the house. To view these terraces the original entrance to the garden was through the Head Gardener's plot and into the Laburnum Arch.

Some mature oaks and beeches gave shelter to the many rhododendron hybrids, usually red, which F. C. Puddle created before and during the Second World War. Using H. *griersonianum* as a parent he produced *Elizabeth, Choremia, Matador, Siren* and *May Day* and his son, Charles Puddle, added many camellias to the plantings. A third generation, Martin Puddle, now leads the six gardeners in maintaining glorious internal and external vistas between and over the azaleas, pieris, embothriums, camellias, rhododendrons and a host of other shrubs.

Crathes

I would have loved to listen in to the arguments which Lord and Lady Burnett had over the planting of this delightful garden near Banchory in Deeside. Lady Burnett favoured herbaceous plants and strong colours as her colourful Pool Garden adjacent to the Castle demonstrates. Lord Burnett was essentially a shrub man and MacDonald, the Head Gardener, would await the day of decision before planting the agreed genera.

The Castle was begun in 1523 and remains intact as a fine back cloth to many of the walks in the garden. The herbaceous borders are very fine and the areas between the early eighteenth century yew hedges are agreeably mixed in their plantings. The latest area to be created by the National Trust is a very successful yellow garden which one New Zealand visitor said "was worth travelling half way round the world to see". Plant lovers, garden designers and casual visitors may all revel in this masterpiece.

Edzell

This small pleasance, dating from 1604, is the second jewel in the Crown of Scottish Gardens for me.

Having travelled widely in Europe, Sir David Lindsay took advantage of a lull in the fighting in Scotland in the first quarter of the seventeenth century to create a Renaissance Pleasance at the mouth of Glen Esk in Angus. Skilled stonemasons from Italy built and carved high red sandstone walls. Above the garden entrance is the motto 'Dum Spiro Spero' (While I breathe, I hope) and this is also cut into the box hedges along with other sayings. On the east wall the Planetary Deities were carved, on the south side the seven Liberal Arts of Grammar,

Rhetoric, Dialectic, Arithmetic, Music, Geometry and Astronomy were portrayed and on the west side the Cardinal Virtues appeared. The inference was that the prosperity and happiness of a truly Renaissance man should be based on his character, on his education and on the heavenly guidance exerted through the mysterious influences of the seven known Planets in their several courses through the Zodiac.

In one corner of this pleasance was a Summer House which acted as a retreat from the busy public rooms and in another corner a cold bath offered refreshment in summer. In the walls were niches where plants displaying the Lindsay colours of blue and white were contained and above the niches nesting holes for birds were provided. A very fine *hortus conclusus* just twenty miles north of Dundee.

Fern Valley

Fern Valley is the wonderful 35-acre garden created at Kloof, some 12 miles inland from Durban in South Africa, by Leslie Riggall. I rate this garden among the very best in the world. I first met Mr. Leslie Riggall at the inaugural meeting of the International Camellia Society at Vincent Square in 1963. He then lived at Titness Park near Windsor and moved to Portugal and then South Africa to grow plants from all over the world. He is the only man outside of Japan to grow every one of E. H. Wilson's 50 Kirume azaleas and he is able to pick a camellia and an orchid on every day in the year.

In a rich acid alluvial top soil and with a warm climate free from frost and snow, a paradise of a garden has been created since 1977. This wonderful garden will be maintained in perpetuity with ample funds from Mr. Leslie Riggall's benevolence. His house has been deliberately built of local fawn coloured stone as a large bungalow which looks down the carefully manicured lawn to the woodland. Perpetual springs provide water for plants and attract gorgeous butterflies and wildlife. The trees are hosts to innumerable orchids, lianas, ferns and jade vines.

Underneath the trees are masses of clivias, agapanthus and rhododendrons. Many of these are the tropical *Vireya* rhododendrons from New Guinea and North Borneo. Leslie Riggall himself collected pollen from R. *lowei* on the slopes of Mount Kinabalu in North Borneo and pollinated other rhododendrons with it.

His camellias have an amazing range and include C. *Chrysantha*, C. *euplebia* and C. *Hongkongensis*. One from Japan, C. *Ringo Taubaki*, has large fruits like rosy apples. Large magnolias were transferred (rather than some of his furniture) from Portugal and M. *Campbellii* will flower when only 4 years old at Kloof. Other trees include Bauhinia *blakeana* and the evergreen Hong-Kong orchid tree, which has fragrant red flowers which can be enjoyed 100 yards away. Allamandas and poinsettias and frangipanis and oranges are just a few of the brilliantly coloured plants which surround the *Kirume* azaleas of the Japanese garden. A Japanese calligrapher has carved the inscription

In this garden are found peace and tranquillity.
When next you visit Natal you should not miss Fern Valley.

Mount Congreve

Mount Congreve is another world class garden near Waterford in Ireland. Over the past 65 years Ambrose Congreve has created a paradise garden along the River Suir on the grandest of scales. New Yorkers ring Mr. Congreve up and enquire when the hundreds of magnolias will be at their best. There are over two hundred Magnolia *campbellii* in many colours, over one hundred M. *campbellii var molli-comata* and scores of M. *sargentiana var robusta*. One form of this magnolia has twenty eight petals. Over five hundred camellias include many of the *Les Jury* hybrids from New Zealand, many Australian hybrids and an enormous range of American cultivars. Every known form of Rhododendron *yakushimanum* is grouped in a large quarry and nearby are thirty different pieris. Thousands of hydrangeas, hundreds of acers and many thousands of rhododendrons stretch for 3 kilometres along the banks of the River Suir. In the spring millions of snowdrops, crocuses, muscari and chionodoxas carpet the ground.

Mr. Ambrose Congreve, who was educated in woodland gardening by Mr. Rothschild at Exbury, is now in his nineties and no longer rides around his garden on a black horse. He has left his house and garden to the nation and his benevolence is most admirable.

Powis

In his excellent 'The History of Gardens' Christopher Thacker writes:

> *Though some may find Bodnant more to their taste, for me Powis is today the most beautiful garden in Britain.*

The terraces below the red sandstone Castle were probably created by William Winde at the end of the seventeenth century. The 1742 engraving by the Buck brothers shows many small standard yew globes which today are huge. William III gave this garden to the Earl of Rochford in the late seventeenth century and in the 1770s William Emes removed the water gardens and landscaped the park land.

Today the terrace plantings of flowering shrubs, clematis, roses and unusual bedding plants are wonderfully colourful. Walking past the Orangery and the third terrace and down to the kitchen garden area and up on to the wilderness ridge for the spectacular view of the terraces and the castle on its rocky outcrop is a splendid perambulation which is so varied. Finally the view northwards from the second terrace with its Van Nost statues to the Breidon hills is delightful.

Preen Manor

Church Preen lies to the west of Much Wenlock in Shropshire. The churchyard boasts a fine old yew tree which has been dated by dendrologists to the seventh century. In Norman times Preen was a Cluniac cell and the monks chose their site well. Sheltered from cold north east winds on a south facing slope with an adequate water supply the site served them well until the Dissolution. I can imagine Henry III visiting the Shropshire cells having assured himself of a plentiful supply of good wine from Bristol. We do not know whether there was a herb garden at Church Preen but we know that a sheep farm occupied the site until Victorian times. Then Norman Shaw was commissioned in 1870 by Arthur Sparrow to build a large Victorian house. This was demolished in the 1920's, though a very fine buttressed wall and an entrance gate remained.

Today Ann Trevor Jones and her late husband Philip have created a superb compartmentalised garden. Like Sissinghurst, it just about has everything and is superior in its vista of Wenlock Edge. To stroll through the cottage garden area, through the beds of the perfumed *Margaret Merril* roses and climb the wooden platform which provides a view over the wall to the Canal garden and Wenlock Edge beyond is only part of the perambulation. It continues through the Chess Garden (formerly an octagon swimming pool) to the potager and then the Nut Walk and the Lion Walk to the old bowling green garden which has many camellias in the woodland. The Rhododendron Walk is between a huge bank of pink (sic)

Rhododendron *ponticum* and leads to the Monks' Bathing Pool and the Water Garden and ancient woodland. Then over the house lawn, past the pebble pool garden to the Stables for a home-made tea. This garden is truly special with its carefully planned and tended compartments and its vistas of the farmed and wooded landscape beyond.

Sutton Place

Sutton Place is near Guildford in Surrey and the house has a rich history. It was built by Sir Richard Weston in the 1520s and today it is the most complete example in England of the transitional style of domestic architecture between the Medieval and the Renaissance periods. Weston had attended Henry VIII on his visit to the Cloth of Gold in France and the chateaux on the Loire. His son, however, was accused by Henry of dallying with Anne Boleyn and was executed in 1536.

After being occupied by Paul Getty in the mid-twentieth century, Sutton Place was bought in 1980 by Mr. Stanley Seeger. When Sir Geoffrey Jellicoe was invited to create a series of garden areas around the house he was greatly impressed by Mr. Seeger's modern art collection. Thus the garden had many references to modern art and included a Surrealist Walk, a setting for Ben Nicholson's white carara marble wall, a swimming pool based on a Paul Miro painting and also a Moss Garden beyond the Paradise Garden. The Moss Garden alluded to the darker elements of the psyche and the octagonal summer house in the corner allowed one to view a woodland area, a farmed landscape and a Gertrude Jekyll inspired herbaceous border. Jellicoe's plan originally provided for a water garden leading up from the River Wey and a garden for musical events.

The present owner, Mr. Koch, has modified Jellicoe's design in several ways. The kitchen garden is now largely given over to roses. The swimming pool has been modified and the Magritte Walk, too, has been changed. Beyond the Ben Nicholson wall a fountain garden has winter flowering shrubs and nearer the summer house an avenue of Acer *pseudo-platanus Brilliantissimum* has been planted. Mr. Koch has also made the Moss Garden into a series of beds with purple and yellow plants.

The Paradise Garden has curving paths between rose and clematis covered arbours with gently rippling fountains. At either side are tunnels of laburnum and honeysuckles. Thus colour, perfume and murmuring water suggest paradise, and the canal near the house may suggest that paradise is not too easy to achieve! To purchase it today would cost £25 millions!

Stourhead

Stourhead is the finest landscaped picture garden today. It lies in Wiltshire where Henry Hoare II created the lake and its several fine buildings from 1745 onwards.

Originally visitors began from the greensand plateau on which the house stands and descended the slope towards the lake. Ahead and floating as it were in the trees across the lake and beyond the Palladian bridge was the Temple of Apollo. At the foot of the slope was a Temple of Flora and across the lake was the Pantheon. Here in centrally heated comfort and refreshed by mulled wine, guests would debate the issues of the day and philosophical questions. From the Pantheon the view across the lake would be towards the village church and the Bristol Cross. This, with the hermitage that was added later, would remind viewers that England had a culture as well as the Romans.

The whole scene is reminiscent of a painting by Claude Lorraine and is ravishingly beautiful at all seasons. Paintings in the house show the scene before the Victorians added conifers and the plantings today are more mixed than Henry Hoare intended. It remains a superb picture landscape garden to visit at any season of the year.

The Valley Gardens at Windsor

My tenth garden is that created by Sir Eric Savill and Thomas Hope Findlay in Windsor Great Park and focuses on Virginia Water. Here the 'Kirume Punchbowl' of evergreen azaleas is ablaze with colour in May. Earlier, acres of hoop petticoat daffodils delight the eye and thousands of camellias, rhododendrons and magnolias provide a scene that even Bhutan, Sikkim and Nepal cannot emulate today.

There are of course many other lovely gardens in the British Isles and a glance through my 'Daylight and Champaign' will reveal fifty of the best garden views. I would especially commend the pagoda area at Kew, the Holford Ride at Westonbirt Arboretum, the herbaceous borders at Arley Hall in Cheshire and at The Priory at Kemerton near Tewkesbury, the Rhododendron 'Fall' at Hergest Croft in Herefordshire, The Great Plat at Hestercombe, the Great Terrace at Iford Manor, the Azaleas at the Dorothy Clive Memorial Garden in Staffordshire, the Pool Garden at Knightshayes, the Peony Border at Penshurst Place, the Winter Border in the Cambridge Botanic Garden and the lovely garden created by Lesley and John Jenkins at Wollerton Hall in Shropshire. As Rudyard Kipling said:

Our England is a Garden
And gardens are not made
By saying "Oh! How beautiful!"
And sitting in the shade.

And, although gardens are partly ephemeral and always changing, they provide much needed refreshment for our spirits in the colours and forms of plants and in the ways in which they are arranged according to the 'genius of the place'. We owe our thanks to all garden owners who open for Charity.

Chapter 9: QUO VADIS?

There have been no purple passages in this slim volume, apart from quotations, no earth shakingly new concepts and no profound prophecies. A young boy walks from Newark-on-Trent to Jasmine Cottage, South Muskham, to enjoy growing plants in a cottage garden. For a time cricket and National Service interrupted his contact with the soil but his studies set him thinking about different garden styles. When he read Milton's 'Paradise Lost' he was confronted with the influence of Nature:

...............the crisped brooks
Ran nectar, visiting each plant, and fed
Flowers worthy of Paradise, which not nice art
In beds and curious knots, but Nature boon
Poured forth profuse on hill, and dale and plains.

When asked to play Sir Toby Belch in Shakespeare's 'Twelth Night' he was asked to hide behind topiary and a box hedge whilst Malvolio strolled in the parterre. And when confronted by Bacon's Essays he was entranced by the opening remarks to the Essay on Gardens —

> *God Almighty first planted a garden. And indeed it is the purest of human pleasures. It is the greatest refreshment to the spirits of man; without which buildings and palaces are but gross handiworks. And a man shall ever see that when ages grow to civility and elegancy, men come to build stately sooner than to garden finely; as if gardening were the greater perfection.*

So gardening was a fine art and a more difficult fine art than architecture. That gave food for thought. And even during my National Service in Palestine as SO2 Education for Gaza Sub District I was made garden steward for the Officers' Mess at Julis by the admirably perceptive Colonel Napier.

After my very happy time at Cambridge from 1948 to 1952, during which time Paddy and I were married at Heswall, a small garden near Blackpool demanded attention. I have outlined how over the years I graduated from annuals at Blackpool to herbaceous and flowering shrubs in Hereford to camellias at Walsall and finally to a small labour saving garden in Worcestershire. Additionally I have always grown vegetables and soft fruit on several allotments.

Garden History was in its infancy when I was first asked to tutor Courses at Birmingham University. When I began in 1972 Gertrude Jekyll was just emerging from obscurity and Norah Lindsay was hardly recognised. About this time Russell Page in his

'The Education of a Gardener' reminded us of Norah Lindsay's genius. He wrote (pp. 203-4)

> *Between the Wars she moved from one country house to the next, gardening and keeping everybody amused and entertained ...... Mrs.Lindsay could by her plantings evoke all the pleasures of a flower garden. She captured the essence of mid-summer with blue and mauve and pink and white and grey or gave the pith of autumn by her sensitive combination of phlox and helenium, montbretias and michaelmas daisies. She lifted her herbaceous plantings into a poetic category and gave it an air of rapture and spontaneity.*

And so I would flesh out this tribute by analysing Norah Lindsay's work at Hidcote, Cliveden, Sutton Courtenay and Blickling Hall. And, of course, I would arrange field visits to these places and to Hestercombe, Barrington Court and Folly Farm to demonstrate Gertrude Jekyll's skill. Over the years I must have taken my classes to well. over 150 gardens.

And abroad, in New York and New Zealand, I enjoyed a period when I gave many lectures. What hyperbole they occasioned! In the local press Mary Carr Hood of New York wrote:

> *What a pleasure to hear a subject presented as perfectly as one could imagine, with such mastery that, even if one had not cared particularly about it before, one would be hooked forthwith and roam hungrily about listening to*

> *anyone who would give tongue on Garden History. But one would be doomed to disappointment that no one could have just the right proportion of information, anecdote and illustration, as Walter Wilde.*

What hyperbole indeed, but very encouraging!

But rather than offer anecdotes about my lectures abroad I wish finally to comment on some principles and traits for the future. Here I find Peter Smither's 'Adventures of a Gardener' very stimulating and wise. He points out in the Introduction to this fine volume that his garden:

> *.......shall be a source of pleasure, not a burden and an anxiety. It must therefore be designed and planted so as to reduce labour to a minimum, and the work involved must diminish as the owner grows old. All plants must therefore be of a permanent character.*

Today in Britain as many as 15 million households have gardens, but the size has dwindled dramatically over recent years. The average size is probably now well under 2000 square feet and this makes it imperative that the plantings should be appropriate. Indeed if I were much younger I would seriously consider opening a nursery which specialised in dwarf shrubs and really dwarf conifers. Most shrubs have a dwarf form, labelled *Nana* or even *pygmea* and, using The Hillier Manual of Trees and Shrubs, these can be easily identified. Of course, the very best forms should be sought. For example, not simply Magnolia *stellata*, but M. *stellata 'Water Lily'*. And, not simply Rhododendron *yakushimanum* (if one has acid soil), but *yakushimanum Koichiro Wada* form or *Percy Wiseman or Yaku Princess*. There is even a dwarf Forsythia called *Arnold Dwarf* and many dwarf Hebes and dwarf willows and so on.

Peter Smithers goes on to say that fragrant and aromatic plants should have preferential admission, as should plants which flower early or late in the year. All told, I find his advice admirable and his adventure at Vico Morcote on Lake Lugano in Switzerland captivating in its advocacy of an ecosystem approach whereby plants tend to support one another.

But in Britain we are faced with a plethora of poor television programmes which give viewers the impression that structure is the secret of creating a garden rather than plants. Of course, a balance is needed between structural elements and plantings. In my present garden I use sculpture and bird baths and urns as focal points and a pergola for climbing plants. But the present trend for so called designers on television is to give the impression that a garden may be created in a few days or weeks. This quick-fix policy defeats much of the object of creating and enjoying a garden. To my mind a garden is not a living room to be decorated and furnished overnight but an evolving sanctuary for humans and other living creatures. Since many of our farmers have destroyed most of the wild flowers and birds in our countryside, gardens have become an essential habitat for their survival. And how I deplore the overuse and advocacy of 'decking' on T.V. programmes. Indeed the substitution of such structures for plants is even suggested by the editor of the R.H.S. Journal, who in January 2001 made a collection of blue sticks the cover picture and commented that they 'created a dramatic optical effect that charmed visitors of all ages to the Jardins de Metes in Canada'. The editor probably congratulated himself on being very *avante garde* but to me his judgement was asinine.

With the decline in the number of allotments available and the reduction in the number of people willing to work regularly on allotments I envisage that more gardens will find room for a potager. Indeed some small gardens may simply become potagers which are decorative as well as productive. If so, they will probably have a geometric design. Four quarters could have carefully laid out and decorative paths in between areas given over to fruit, flowers, vegetables and herbs. As John Evelyn observed in the seventeenth century, 'A garden is a voluptuous and empty speculation without some tincture of medicine'. By which he advocated, not simply thyme and sage and rosemary, but many other interesting herbs. The potagers at Barnsley House and Preen Manor offer many ideas for interesting plantings. Ruby chard, red cabbages, blue borage, variegated lettuce, standard gooseberries, apples trained into goblet shapes and sweet peas on tripods all add interest. Moreover marrows may be trained on pergolas with gaillardias at the base to add colour (see Illustration 6). Standard roses such as *Little Pet* can add height and alcoves with seats may be covered with golden hops or the thornless roses *Zephirine Drouhin* and

Kathleen Harrop, with clematis *Perle D'Azure* for additional colour.

Gardens will continue to echo the personality and the life style of the owners. Some will prefer 'minimalist serenity' whilst others will revel in the considered disorder of the traditional cottage garden. Some will forego grass and replace it with gravel and dwarf conifers. Some will revel in sunset colours while others prefer pastel shades and large areas of foliage. But most gardens will act as a refuge from stress and an opportunity to create beauty.

Erasmus' dictum can hardly be bettered:

> *A garden is a place dedicated to the honourable pleasures of rejoicing the eye, refreshing the nose and renewing the spirit.*

Epilogue

I would like to think that my lectures and courses in Garden History over the past 30 years have, as Seneca once said, 'Instructed, Delighted and Moved' my class members in many enjoyable ways. I have learnt much from them and from garden owners who allowed us to visit and been greatly encouraged. In the Autumn of 2001, for example, I ran a Course at Little Witley on 'The English Landscape Garden' and one member, Lynne Symonds, wrote on her Christmas card

> *Just a note to thank you again for a most entertaining Course. Wednesday evenings will not be the same and you will be sorely missed by us all. Lecturers invariably have a wealth of knowledge but not all possess your ability to convey it with such passion, conviction and good humour. Your lectures were so warm, friendly and entertaining and your infectious enthusiasm will inspire us all to find out more and visit the places mentioned. For students like me, who are merely keen to add to their knowledge of a particular subject, this was a particular delight — an opportunity to be educated within a relaxing and companionable environment. I sincerely hope that the University will send you back to us again.*

What a privilege to have such appreciative class members and friends! In conclusion, I would like to record that two of my Birmingham students — Mrs. Irene Cohn and Miss Joyce Baynham — have attended every single Course that I have run at the University since 1972. Their loyalty and dedication to Garden History is remarkable.

In his 'Adventures of a Gardener' Peter Smithers records how a young Indian woman advised him that old people should 'turn inwards away from material things'. I find it difficult to follow this ancient Buddhist wisdom so long as I can see beautiful flowers and leaves in gardens. That trite remark 'Say it with flowers' is also a wise comment. For what words can conjure up the beauty of your favourite flower newly opened? And as John Wesley wrote 'As flowers their opening leaves display, And glad drink in the solar fire', so I hope that your experience of the difficult but rewarding fine art of gardening will make life more worth living when other comforts fail. Even a gardening nobody may find enormous pleasure in sharing the love of gardens with others.

May my children, Deborah, Philip and Adam, and my grandchildren Hannah, Polly, Eleanor, Naomi, Benjamin, Oliver and Annabel, find similar, or even greater satisfaction from the 'purest of pleasures'.

BIBLIOGRAPHY

Anderson, E.B. (1961) *Camellias*, Blandford

Anderson, E.B. (1973) *Severn Gardens*, Michael Joseph

Anderson, E.B. (1963) *Splendour of Earth*, G.Philip

Banks, Elizabeth (1991) *Creating Period Gardens*, Phaidon

Batey, Mavis (1989) *The Historic Gardens of Oxford and Cambridge*, MacMillan

Bowles, E.A. (1997) *My Garden in Spring* (*reprint*), Timber Press

Brown, Jane (1990) *The English Garden in our Time*, Antique Collectors' Club

Brown, Jane (1982) *Gardens of a Golden Afternoon*, Van Nostrand

Campbell-Culver, M. (2001) *The Origin of Plants*, Headline

Cane, Percy (1956) *The Earth is My Canvas*, Methuen

Clark, H. F. (1948) *The English Landscape Garden*, Pleiades

Clarke, Ethne (1989) *Hidcote*, Michael Joseph

Clausen R. R. and Ekstrom N. H. (1989) *Perennials for American Gardens*, New York: Random House

Clifford, Derek (1966)*A History of Garden Design*, Faber

Crowe, Sylvia (1958) *Garden Design*. Country Life

Desmond, R. (1999) *Sir Joseph Hooker*, Antique Collectors' Club

Dutton, Ralph (1950) *The English Garden*, Batsford

Elliott, Brent. (1986) *Victorian Gardens*, Batsford

Fleming, Laurence & Gore Alan (1988) *The English Garden*, Spring Books

Gibson, N. (1988) *The Rose Gardens of England*, Collins

Gray, Ronald (1984) *Cambridge Gardens*, Pevensey Press

Hadfield, Miles. (1960) *A History of British Gardening*, Spring Books

Harvey, John (1990) *Medieval Gardens*, Batsford

Hayden, Peter (1989) *Biddulph Grange*, George Philip

Heron, M. (1999) *The Gardens of Ireland,* Collins and Brown

Hillier, E. G. (1956) *The Manual of Trees and Shrubs*, David and Charles

Hinde, Thomas (1986) *Capability Brown*, Hutchinson

Hobhouse, Penelope (1986) *Private Gardens of England*, Weidenfeld and Nicolson

Hunt, John Dixon and Willis, Peter (eds.) (1975) *The Genius of the Place*, Elek

Hussey, Christopher (1967) *English Gardens and Landscapes*, Country Life

Huxley, Anthony (1978) *An Illustrated History of Gardening*, Paddington Press

Jaques, David (1983) *Georgian Garden*, Batsford

Jellicoe, Geoffrey and Susan in Goode, Patrick and Lancaster, Michael eds. (1991) *The Oxford Companion to Gardens*, O.U.P.

Jellicoe, Geoffrey and Susan (1987) *The Landscape of Man*, Thames and Hudson

Joyce, David (ed.) (1986) *Garden Styles*, Pyramid Books

King, Ronald (1979) *The Quest for Paradise*, Whittet Books

Lacey, Stephen (1996) *Gardens of the National Trust*, N.T.

Lamb, K. and Bowe, P. (1995) *A History of Gardening in Ireland*, Dublin: Stationery Office

Lees-Milne, Alvide and Verey, Rosemary (eds.) (1983) *The English Woman's Garden*, Chatto and Windus

Lees-Milne, Alvide and Verey, Rosemary (eds.) (1982) *The English Man's Garden*, Allen Lane

Lees—Milne, Alvide and Verey, Rosemary eds. (1987) *The New Englishwoman's Garden*, Chatto and Windus

Lloyd, C. (2001) *Colour for Adventurous Gardens*, BBC Books

McLean, Teresa (1989) *Medieval English Gardens*, Barrie and Jenkins

Maitland, S. and Matthews, P. (2000) *Gardens of Illusion*, Cassell

Massingham, B. (1974) *Turn on the Fountains*, Gollancz

Mosser, Monique, Teyssot (1991) *The History of Garden Design*, Thames and Hudson

Nitschke, Gunter (1993) *Japanese Gardens*, Koln: Benedikt Taschen

Ottewill, David (1989) *The Edwardian Garden*, Yale University Press

Page, Russell (1985) *The Education of a Gardener*, Penguin

Palmer, A. and B. (1990) *Some Shropshire Gardens*, Shropshire Books

Plumptre, George (1993) *The Garden Makers*, Pavilion

Rix, M. (1985) *The Art of Botanical Illustration*, Bracken Books

Robinson, William (1984) *The English Flower Garden*, New York: Amaryllis Press

Rogers, E. B. (2001) *Landscape Design: a Cultural and Architectural History*, Harry N. Abrams

Roper, Lanning (1962) *The Gardens of the Royal Park at Windsor*, Chatto and Windus

Sanders, R. (1988) *The Apple Book*, Phaidon

Scott-James, Anne (1987) *Sissinghurst*, Michael Joseph

Smithers, P. (1995) *Adventures of a Gardener*, Harvill

Stearn, W. T. (ed.) (1999) *John Lindley*, Antique Collectors' Club

Stearn, W. T. (2000) *Botanical Latin*, David and Charles

Strong, Roy (1979) *The Renaissance Garden in England.*

Stroud, Dorothy (1975) *Capability Brown*, Faber

Thacker, Christopher (1979) *The History of Gardens*, Croom Helm

Thacker, Christopher (1994) *The Genius of Gardening*, Weidenfeld and Nicolson,

Thomas, G. S. (1979) *Gardens of the National Trust*, Weidenfeld and Nicolson

Thomas, G.S. (ed). (1987) *A Garden of Roses*, Michael Joseph

Thorpe, H. (1965) *Cmnd 4166*, HMSO

Turner, Tom (1986) *English Garden Design*, Antique Collectors' Club

Verey. R. (1984) *Classic Garden Design*, Viking

Verney, Peter (undated) *The Gardens of Scotland*, Batsford

Wakefield, G.R. (1964) *Camellias for Every Garden*, Collingridge

Wallinger, H. (2000) *Gertrude Jekyll's Lost Garden*, Antique Collectors' Club

Webber, Roy (1975) *Percy Cane: Garden Designer*, J. Bartholmew

Whittle, Elizabeth (1992) *The Historic Gardens of Wales*, HMSO

Wilde, W. (1997) *Daylight and Champaign*, The Bassett Press

Wilde, W. (1983) *The Evolution of Landscape Parks and Pleasure Grounds along the Trent Valley in Staffordshire, 1750-1850*, University of Birmingham Thesis

Woodbridge, Kenneth (1965) 'Henry Hoare's Paradise', in *The Art Bulletin of the College Art Association of America*, March 1965, (reprinted by the National Trust)